AUTUMN IN PRISON AND OTHER POEMS

F.W. HARVEY

YELLOW LEAF PRESS

ABOUT THE AUTHOR

F.W. Harvey (born in Gloucestershire in 1888) was an English poet, solicitor, and BBC broadcaster known for his poetry written during confinement in World War I German prisons. His most popular poem, "Ducks," was written in prison after he saw a fellow inmate draw ducks in a pond on the wall using chalk. Harvey's political views were Bohemian, and he worked for the poor as a defense solicitor. Though honorable, this practice financially failed, yet he found success as a broadcaster due to his powerful voice. Still, he gave away his services and income and was not materialistic. He married Anne Kane in 1921 and had two children, Eileen Anne (1922) and Patrick (1925). He died in 1957 and was buried at Minsterworth. Harvey is now remembered as a war-poet, and his war poetry is anthologized in war poetry collections.

CONTENTS

HEAVEN

"Take me, then," he said to the angel, "upon this great journey to Heaven."

The angel touched his eyelids.

"Where, then, is Hell?" asked the man.

The spirit pointed out a bored-looking man quite near the throne.

"But he is in Heaven," protested the mortal.

"Even so, but he does not know it," replied the angel.

AUTUMN IN PRISON

Here where no tree changes,
  Here in a prison of pine,
I think how Autumn ranges
  The country that is mine.

There—rust upon the chill breeze—
  The woodland leaf now whirls;
There sway the yellowing birches
  Like dainty dancing girls.

Oh, how the leaves are dancing
  With Death at Lassington!
And Death is now enhancing
  Beauty I walked upon.

The roads with leaves are littered,
  Yellow, brown, and red.
The homes where robins twittered
  Lie ruin; but instead

Gaunt arms of stretching giants
   Stand in the azure air,
Cutting the sky in pattern
   So common, yet so fair.

The heart is kindled by it,
   And lifted as with wine,
In Lassington and Highnam—
   The woodlands that were mine.

DUCKS

(To F.M., Who drew them in Holzminden Prison)

I

From troubles of the world I turn to ducks,
Beautiful comical things
Sleeping or curled
Their heads beneath white wings
By water cool,
Or finding curious things
To eat in various mucks
Beneath the pool,
Tails uppermost, or waddling
Sailor-like on the shores
Of ponds, or paddling
- Left! Right! - with fanlike feet
Which are for steady oars
When they (white galleys) float
Each bird a boat
Rippling at will the sweet

Wide waterway . . .
When night is fallen you creep
Upstairs, but drakes and dillies
Nest with pale water-stars.
Moonbeams and shadow bars,
And water-lilies:
Fearful too much to sleep
Since they've no locks
To click against the teeth
Of weasel and fox.
And warm beneath
Are eggs of cloudy green
Whence hungry rats and lean
Would stealthily suck
New life, but for the mien
The hold ferocious mien
Of the mother-duck.

II

Yes, ducks are valiant things
On nests of twigs and straws,
And ducks are soothy things
And lovely on the lake
When that the sunlight draws
Thereon their pictures dim
In colours cool.
And when beneath the pool
They dabble, and when they swim
And make their rippling rings,
0 ducks are beautiful things!
But ducks are comical things:—
As comical as you.

Quack!
They waddle round, they do.
They eat all sorts of things,
And then they quack.
By barn and stable and stack
They wander at their will,
But if you go too near
They look at you through black
Small topaz-tinted eyes
And wish you ill.
Triangular and clear
They leave their curious track
In mud at the water's edge,
And there amid the sedge
And slime they gobble and peer
Saying 'Quack! quack!'

III

When God had finished the stars and whirl of coloured suns
He turned His mind from big things to fashion little ones;
Beautiful tiny things (like daisies) He made, and then
He made the comical ones in case the minds of men
Should stiffen and become
Dull, humourless and glum,
And so forgetful of their Maker be
As to take even themselves - quite seriously.
Caterpillars and cats are lively and excellent puns:
All God's jokes are good - even the practical ones!
And as for the duck, 1 think God must have smiled a bit
Seeing those bright eyes blink on the day He fashioned it.
And he's probably laughing still at the sound that came out of
    its bill!

NOVEMBER

He he hanged himself-the Sun.
     He dangles
A scarecrow in thin air.

He is dead for love-the Sun;
     He who in forest tangles
Wooed all things fair.

That great lover-the Sun,
     Now spangles
The wood with blood-stains.

He has hanged himself—the Sun.
     How thin he dangles
In these gray rains!

THESE FIELDS

Dream not the English meadows dead.
I heard some fields in Gloucestershire
Whispering ere the sun had kist
Their level faces clean of mist.
And very sweet it was to hear
The secret words they said
Clear-spoken by green little lips
Of grass with dew upon the tips.
And mingling in the gossip spoke

With softly-rustling leaves the oak;
Elms too, and the gray willows that look
Into the little twisting brook,
And a garrulous old scythe that lay
Under a bramble hidden away,
Together with a drinking-horn
Fashioned long ere I was born. . . .
They spoke the language they had heard
Since they had listened to any word.
They were more English than our tongue:

Old already when words were young.

They said that life ran much the same
Or ever Caesar's army came.
Norman and Saxon were but words.
The men went, the men came;
They took them, but forgot the name.
They took them, these mild fields, these birds,
These streams, these oaks, this grass, and wrought
Within their minds an English thought.
And moulding thus, they made amends
For bloodshed and much labour: gave
Content of thought and food to friends:
Shade to labourers and to lovers:
Water to wash to the world's ends
The care a living man discovers,
Ind all anxiety and fear
Which life and love may bring too near.

Thus to an immemorial plan
They fashioned and kept the Englishman
A coin of England ringing true:
A bloom of England under blue
Or dark skies: thus for many a day
Past. *And so still purpose they.*

SEPTEMBER

She walketh like a ghost,
  Lovely and gray
And faint, faint, faint . . .
  Ere Autumn's host
Of colours gay
  Breaks on the year, September
Comes sighing her soft plaint,
  'Remember!'

Remember what? All fair
  Warm loves now wan:
All fleet, fleet, fleet
  Flowers in the hair
Of Summers gone!
  Though fruit break rosy, of these
Are her most sweet
  Sad memories.

Most faint and tender
  Music awaketh,

sighing, sighing, sighing
  A voice to lend her.
Surely it breaketh
  Even Death's heart, as he goes
To gather in Summer's long-dying
  Last rose.

So drifting like a ghost,
  Lovely with dream
And faint, faint, faint,
  Sighing ' remember,' almost
September did seem
  My gray soul's image, as she
Whispered over that plaint
  So musically!

A PRAYER

O Lord, within my heart for ever,
Set this sweet shape of land and winding river,
That I may taste their comfort till I die,
And feed upon them in Eternity.

STARS

Nothing more friendly—old,
   Man knows on earth, than these
Bright shapes that shepherds and sailors have blessed
       In fields: on seas.

Yet millions of strange years
   They, set in Heaven's dark face,
Have sung of loneliness, dancing
       To empty space.

IF WE RETURN

If we return, will England be
Just England still to you and me?
The place where we must earn our bread?
We, who have walked among the dead.
And watched the smile of agony,

And seen the price of Liberty,
Which we have taken carelessly
From other hands. Nay, we shall dread,
        If we return,

Dread lest we hold blood-guiltily
The things that men have died to free.
Oh, English fields shall blossom red
For all the blood that has been shed
By men whose guardians are we,
        If we return.

SWIFT BEAUTY

Wind that is in orchards
   Playing with apple-trees
Soon will be leagues away
   In the old rookeries.

Vaguely it arises,
   Swiftly it hurries hence:—
Like sudden beauty
   Blown over sense:

Like all unheeded
   Beautiful things that pass
Under the leaves of life,
   Just touching the grass.

ADOLESCENCE

This tender scorn, this majesty of weather,
   Mocks all we dream or do.
Its silent message like an eagle's feather
   Flutters from out the blue
      Shaming all high endeavour,
      Making our labour vain for ever and ever.

Oh, that a quest noble enough could be found
   To match such scornful beauty!
Oh, that, with feet set firm on common ground,
   Man might attain the height of heavenly duty:
      That the green hedge into green fire
      Would flame and burn our world to Heaven's desire!

HE PASSETH BY

Christ Jesus Who lived long ago
Far from streets where we men go,
The fiercest and the tenderest was
Of any born. He loved the grass
And all tiny things that creep
In that little forest to hide and sleep.
He worked with sailors on their ships,
And stilled for them the storm. With whips
He drove from church those cruel old
Fat priests, whose mildewed words and cold
Froze up like icicles and killed
The happy common life God willed
Should bubble up in man and woman.
Christ's wise love it was so human
He saved a harlot they would stone
And showed that *her* sin was their own.
And 'sin no more,' He said to *all*;
Sinless Himself, He came to all
Sot, harlot, murderer, and thief
Into His fold. Their tears of grief

Were pearls upon the crown that He
Wore upon earth invisibly.
He died, and rose—and is forgotten.
And now the world hangs like a rotten
Apple upon the Tree of Life.
For men are steeped in deadly strife,
And, weak with hate, and blind with pride,
On their own cruelty crucified.

UNSTABLE

A hill in steadfast loveliness
Wears the morning's misty dress;
Puts on the sunlight's golden crown;
Dons a starry or purple gown;
But keeps against all weather-fate
Its own form inviolate;
And such is the happy destiny
Of some men. But alas for me,
I would be steadfast as the hill
But am as water running still
The path it must. I would be frozen
In ecstasy of some shape chosen:—
Whether of joy, whether of pain,
Matters little. I would remain
Finely myself, but consecrate
To beauty be it love or hate.
But when by any known device
Was water fixed unless in ice?
I dimple into good. I eddy
Back into evil, bravely ready

To change again, reflecting ever
My mood:—but my desire, never.
O sooner shall the honey bees
Forsake Spring-blossom, than I freeze;
And sooner shall a playing fountain
Turn to rock, than I to mountain.

TO THE DEVIL ON HIS
APPALLING DECADENCE

Satan, old friend and enemy of man;
Lord of the shadows and the sins whereby
We wretches glimpse the sun in Virtue's sky
Guessing at last the wideness of His plan
Who fashioned kid and tiger, slayer and slain,
The paradox of evil, and the pain
Which threshes joy as with a winnowing fan:

Satan, of old your custom 'twas at least
To throw an apple to the soul you caught
Robbing your orchard. You, before you wrought
Damnation due and marked it with the beast,
Before its eyes were e'en disposed to dangle
Fruitage delicious. And you would not mangle
Nor maul the body of the dear deceased.

But you were called familiarly "Old Nick"—
The Devil, yet a gentleman you know!
Relentless—true, yet courteous to a foe.

Man's soul your traffic was. You would not kick
His bloody entrails flying in the air.
Oh, "Krieg ist Krieg," we know, and "C'est la guerre!"
But Satan, don't you feel a trifle sick?

WHAT WE THINK OF

Walking round our cages like the lions at the Zoo,
We think of things that we have done, and things we mean
    to do:
Of girls we left behind us, of letters that are due,
Of boating on the river beneath a sky of blue,
Of hills we climbed together—not always for the view.

Walking round our cages like the lions at the Zoo,
We see the phantom faces of you, and you, and you,
Faces of those we loved or loathed—oh every one we knew!
And deeds we wrought in carelessness for happiness or rue,
And dreams we broke in folly, and seek to build anew,—
Walking round our cages like the lions at the Zoo.

FORSAKEN

Silent it comes
       With no dark pageantry,
Or drums.
Naught's to see.
       Only the horrible shadow bends
Over me.
Where wait ye, friends?
       Not even Satan with me!
So all ends.
And will ye
       Also forsake this head,
My dreams? They flee.
Discomforted
       My very self has flown.
I am dead,
Less than alone,
       Less than a worm, a tree,
A stone.

TO THE MAKERS OF LAUGHTER

Though life with sorrow's woven,
And Hope be liar proven,
    Yet Laughter shall remain,
And, deeper than man's reason,
Acquit the earth of treason;
    The heavens of disdain.

A toast to you, old Francis
Rabelais whose spirit dances
    Like light upon the wave
Of trouble tumbling round me:
For surely had it drowned me
    But for your jesting brave!

Dan Chaucer, hail! Your dirt is
Than our soap cleaner. Surtees,
    Your clumsy English jig
Is lighter than our dancing
And merrier. Set them prancing—
    John Jorrocks, Huntsman Pigg!

You sit there broadly grinning,
And often maybe sinning;
   Yet kings o'er all the rest,
Whose solemn looks of yearning
Disgust the saints; whose learning
   Is lighter than a jest.

All praise, high-hearted shakers
Of hell!—Good laughter-makers
   Earth's salt you are, and were!
Who seeing, clear, life's sorrow,
Yet mock it down, and borrow
   Strong courage of despair.

CLOUD MESSENGERS

You clouds that with the wind your warden
    Flying toward the Channel go,
Or ever the frost your fruit shall harden
    To hail and sleet and driving snow,
Go seek one sunny old sweet garden—
    An English garden that I know.

Therein perchance my Mother, straying
    Among her dahlias, shall see
Your rainy gems in sunlight swaying
    On flower of gold and emerald tree.
    Then in her heart feel suddenly
Old love and laughter, like sunshine playing
    Through tears of memory.

THE STRANGER

It happened in a blood-red hell ringed round with golden
        weather;
Walking in khaki through a trench he came,
When life was death, and wounded men and great shells
        screamed together:
I did not know his name.
But so white-faced and wan, we talked a little while together
Amongst dead men, and timbers black with flame.

"What would you do with life again," asks he, "if one could
        give it?"
"No use to talk when life is done," I say.
"But, by the living God, if He should grant me life I'd live it
Kinder to man, truer to God each day."

Flame and the noise of doom devoured the words, and for a
        while
Senseless I lay.... Then,
Oh, then as in a dream I saw the stranger with a smile
Moving towards me over the dead men.

Red, red were his hands and feet and a great hole in his side,
Yet glory seemed to blaze about his head;
"Kinder to man, truer to God," he whispered, and then died;
Falling down, arms outspread.
Ere darkness fell upon me with the faintness and the pain,
I saw a mangled body lying prone
Upon the earth beside me. But what I can't explain
Is—*The stretcher-bearers found me quite alone.*

But, howsoe'er it happened, it matters not at last,
Since God's dear Son came down to earth and died
In bloodshed, and the darkness of clouds that groaned aghast;
With pierced hands and a great wound in His side.

It is not in my heart to hate the pleasant sins I leave.
Earth's passion flames within me fierce and strong.
But this is like a shadow ever rising up to thieve
Sin's pleasures, and the lure of every pattern lust can weave,
And charm of all things that can do Him wrong.

THE ROUND POOL

When high flies the swallow
Fine weather will follow
And to this green hollow
      Will little boys come,

And heedless of mother
And grim elder brothers,
Schoolmaster and others
      Who sit stern and glum,

To play round the water
With shout and shrill laughter
Till sunset and after,
      Forgetful of all;

While I never heeding
Time's growth and rank seeding,
Mouse-like do sit feeding
      On joys past recall,

And hark to a singing
Of hours fleetly winging
To nowhere, yet bringing
        For ever new joy,

When earth was a chalice
Of wonder, not malice,
And time but a palace
        Built for a boy.

EARLY MARCH

Thin panes of ice upon
    The puddles in the track
Slanted fires of the sun
    Fling back

Into the dazzled eyes
    Of a whistling boy,
Who mocks the thrush's twice
    Repeated stave of joy.

High on a warm wall's top
    A curled cat lies gray,
Drinking to the last drop
    The golden cream of day.

Her eyes, and an old door
    New-painted green,
Are the only verdure
    Yet to be seen.

But spring is now in the air,
    As bird and boy well know:
And here, and there,
    Trees too. For though

Along the muddy track
    On either hand,
Delicate and black,
    The elms stand,

Where the gray rapiers clash
    In the wind—lo!
Black buds are on their points. The Ash
    But plays with his foe.

The old swordsman's hand has lost
    Its stern and beautiful
Strength. His sword of frost
    Is blunted and dull:

And his power broken; as birds
    And boys well see
Who whistle Spring's old words
    Of rivalry.

CHRISTMAS IN PRISON

Outside, white snow
And freezing mire.
The heart of the house
Is a blazing fire!

Even so whatever hags do ride
His outward fortune, withinside
The heart of a man burns Christmastide!

SPRING 1924

Spring came by water to Broadoak this year.
I saw her clear.
Though on the earth a sprinkling
Of snowdrops shone, the unwrinkling
Bright curve of Severn River
Was of her gospel first giver.
Like a colt new put to pasture it galloped on;
And a million
Small things on its back for token
Of her coming it bore. A broken
Hawthorn floated green,
Gem-bright upon the sheen
Of the moving water. There past
Hay-wisps which showed the fast
Of winter was over for cattle,
Who needed no longer battle
For food in some far meadow.
Soft as shadow
There glided past a skiff,
Heavy with mended nets for salmon. If

Spring dreamed
Lazily in Earth's half-frozen blood,
On Sever's flood
Her presence bravely gleamed.
Yea, all who sought her
Might see, wondering, how Spring walked the water.

NOW SWEET NIGHT

Now sweet night
   Stealeth upon
The yet bright
   But drowsy sun,

His hot crimson
   Form to busk
Cool in damson-
   Coloured dusk.

Her mystery
   With dark leaves
Of each tall tree
   She interweaves:

Next, launches
   Starry ships
Over the branches:—
   Even so slips

Now sweet night
　With dreams down,
And the day's light
　Is overthrown.

So softly, so
　Sweetly, Death,
Come thou,
　With thy cool breath:

Thy dream unhasting:
　Thy dusky mood
Of everlasting
　Quietude.

PONDERING HER LOVELINESS

Pondering her loveliness,
      I saw the world of sense dissolve, to take
Swift beauty in a cup
      Brimming with dreams.

Lo, as earth faded,
Line into line wondrously marrying,
Crept forth her loveliness.
      And else was nothing.

How frail are dreams!
The crackle of a stick beneath the heel:
The trilling of a bird,
      Shatter them, scatter them!

BEAUTY

(To Sir Edward Elgar)

Out of life's flow and ebb,
 Past the last lit star,
Which, like a golden fly,
Flutters in time's dark web:
 Lonely and far
The place that I would find,
A lighted inn of the mind:
 Far, yet not strange.

No man yet hath seen it,
 Though fair it is to see.
None hear it
 Though of builded song it be.
It shall outlast all heavens,
 Though light as the foam.
 It is my home,
Though never was I near it.

A bed is ready,
 A place of utter rest, there:
Out of time's eddy,
 And the grooves of the heavy stars:
Beyond the golden gateways of the sun.
 And the brain's iron bars.
 Derelict dreams all nest there. . . .
  By a single light
   March I, and have marched
   Under the arched
  Darkness of night,
   Upon my way.
   This shall not lead me astray
  Though all guides fail me:—
Beauty the star of God, His herald, His burning thought,
Web of that song wherein each turning world
Is caught.
Thus do I hail thee,
Banner of God unfurled!

COUNTRY LOVE-SONG

The days between the days we meet
    What be um more than shadows—
Like the strong zun do cast along
    From elms over the meadows?

Those days whereon we meet, my sweet,
    Being zuns both bright and strong,
Make in their rays all other days
    Fall just zo black and long!

THREE SPARROWS ON A SPRAY

Three sparrows clustered on a spray of
    hawthorn, gray with sprinkled hoar
Have shut out right and shut out wrong, and made
    delight to sing her song,—
The song that is all quietness.
They've shut out weariness and din, and dreariness
    and thought of sin.
They've closed a door within my brain, and poured
    disdain on weariness.

The bramble scorns, with all her thorns, our roads
    of care to ramble.
The hawthorn spray finds still a way above the
    griefs of men.
Unflecked with thought of *would* and *ought*, by
    could and *should* unchecked,
Goes Nature all unconsciously, joyously and silently,
Nor ponders, nor wanders the worlds beyond her ken.

Our songs are gongs to summon up a host of warring fancies.

Our quiet books still caw like rooks or ravens o'er the dead.
A bowstring is our questioning which looseth
    poisoned arrows.
Our reason is treason.
Our wisdom never dances.
But the hawthorn spray is merry with the weight of
    three brown sparrows,
Who peck a single berry shining bright and red,
Who close a door within the brain and pour disdain
    on weariness,
Who show a world to dreariness and clamour deaf
    and blind:
Untarnished joys not rusty with a breath of noise,
    nor dusty with
Philosophy's vain sweepings in the chambers of
    the mind:
And dreams that live unspoken, unbroken and
    apart,
In a world of silent wonder long-forgotten, buried under
The sad half-world of warfare which is named a
    human heart.

CONSOLATOR AFFLICTORUM

"Must ever I be so
—Yellow and old?" you asked,
"With living overtasked,
Ugly, and racked with pains?"
I answered, "Even so,
Dearest; yet love remains."

'OUT OF THE MOUTHS OF BABES—'

Two children in my garden playing around
    A robin cruelly dead, in Summer hours.
I watched them get a trowel, and heap the mound,
    And bury him, and scatter over flowers.

And when their little friend was laid away,
    In lack of burial service over the dead
Before those two grave children turned to play:—
    'I hope he 'll have a happy *dead* life!' one said.

What more was there to say for bird or beast?
    What more for any man is there to say?
What can we wish *them* better, as with priest
    And choir we ring the cross on Armistice Day?

BEGGARS

You without heed or pity
    Of men who slink
From city to city
    Lacking food, lacking drink:
        Fluttering
       Foul tatter;
        Muttering
      Poverty's whining patter:
        For alms
       stretching palms . . .

When you have died:
    When tramp and king
Lie gowned alike in emerald, and crowned
    Golden with buttercup:
    Be beggars still! Rise up
And beg the Crucified
    That He forgive the world your suffering!

GHOSTS

A very old woman sat over the fire
    One came to the door
Whose tap loud-echoed. She did not hear.
    He crossed the threshold o'er.

'Come with me, ancient mother,' he beckoned.
    'Nay, I be too old to move;
Where do 'e want ver I to journey?'
    Croaked she. Death bent above.

'You had ('twas many a year now past)
    A son dread waters drowned.'
At that the aged body started
    To twist herself around.

'He sailed with me, I loved him better
    Than any.' 'Then ye lie!'
Flashed back her answer. 'For nobody
    Loved him so well as I.'

'To you I bear a message
    And a message that is his . . .'
'Tell it, tell it, sweet Death!' 'Nay, mother;
    First—a kiss.'

Then the old trembling woman uprose
    From her low seat, and
Gave her lips to the stranger,
    Her lips; her hand.

'You are too old to journey, mother,
    I'll stay with you here instead.'
'Who speaks?' 'Your son, your dear son,
    mother,—Dead to the dead.'

LONELINESS

Oh where's the use to write?
What can I tell you, dear?
Just that I want you so
Who are not near.
Just that I miss the lamp whose blessed light
Was God's own moon to shine upon my night,
And newly mourn each new day's lost delight:
Just—oh, it will not ease my pain—
That I am lonely
Until I see you once again,
You—you only.

IN LODGINGS

Nothing sounds in the house
    Except the owner's snore.
A little silent mouse
    Flits over the floor
Spring-cleaned so proudly
    By the woman whom
We hear doing nothing so loudly
    In the next room.

He is doing a lot . . .
    With a frisk
He scales her marmalade pot;
    Taking his risk
Of falling headlong into
    That sticky heaven of his.
She sleeps. It would be a sin to
    Disturb his ecstasies!

And so I pause in scribbling,
    Lest, turning a sheet over,

I should stop his sweet nibbling
    At the pot's cover.
Dishonest, no doubt,
    For it isn't my jam,
And should not have been left out
    —Nor the ham!

But here are we three:—
    I, and the mouse,
And the snoring landlady
    Of the house,
Each assisting each
    (Though I alone know it)
Laughing patience to teach
    An impatient poet,

Whose little pen would scrape
    Like a mouse's nail
The cloths which drape
    Joys that not fail,
In a house where Death
    (That landlady so grim)
Snores yet, but tarrieth
    Not long to trap *him*.

JOE'S LUCK

Joe rested by the gate, and thought that of any
   Life open to a man, by far the worst
Was a poor drunken tramp's whose last brown penny
   Had gone on beer: wherefore he roundly curse
Man, God, and devil indiscriminately,
   And cursed the gate, and cursed the careless fool
Who'd left it banging, also the dark tree
   That threw queer shadow over the moon-bright pool.

Queer shadow truly!—for upon it dangled
   The man who had not paused to close that gate.
Dead at the end of a cord he hung there, strangled . . .
   Joe cried aloud, and all his thought of hate
Changed into abject terror as he ran,
   He knew not where, out of that tree's dark shadow,
Out of the flapping shadow of the man
   That crossed the pool and sprawled upon the meadow.

But in his breathless running, suddenly
   He halted. For there came into his head

That that which he had seen upon the tree
   Was haply not yet dead.
So timidly he turned him back, and stood
   Fearfully gazing, ere he snatched a flint
To sever that tough cord as best he could.
   The keen stone marked his hands with many a dint.

Down came the dreadful body, and lay humped
   And horrible on the ground beside him. Joe
Put ear to the cold breast, but, save the thump
   Of his own heart, heard nothing at all: so
After a while concluded (which was true)
   The man was dead; and, something bolder grown,
Ceased rubbing him to search the pockets through.
   'Money's a thing a dead man doesn't own.'

So argued Joe, as into his own pocket
   He slid the silver. Then a while he paused
Furtively fingering over a gold locket.
   'Maybe,' he mused, 'that pictured woman caused His death.
He put it back again. A cloud
   Passed overhead, and made the moonlight dim.
An owl in some near thicket hooted loud.
   Thought Joe, 'I'll not take what belongs to *him*?'

'Yes, he can keep the shillings too,' he said;
   'Though I'm the fool to let him, seeing what
I done for him in case he wasn't dead;
   It being too as how I 'haven't got
A blinking 'a'penny on me.' The sweet scent
   Of earth arose. Again the moon did show.
Shutting the gate behind him as he went,
   'It ain't too bad to be *alive*,' mused Joe.

ON PAINSWICK BEACON

Here lie counties five in a waggon wheel.
There quick Severn like a silver eel
Wriggles through pastures green and pale stubble.
There, sending up its quiet coloured bubble
Of earth, May Hill floats on a flaming sky.
And, marvelling at all, forgetting trouble,
Here—home again—stand I!

TO KATHLEEN, AT CHRISTMAS

Kings of the East did bring their gold
A nd jewels unto the cattle fold.
The angel's song was heard by men
"Holy! holy! holy!" then.
Little and weak in the manger He lay
Even as you in a cradle to-day;
Even as you did the Christ-child rest
Nestling warm in His mother's breast.

Gütersloh,
December 1916.

VERSES

(On the unveiling of the 5th Gloucestershire Regiment's War
Memorial)

Here, to a thousand men who loved this land,
 And breathed its quiet air, and laughed, and played
 And met with death like lovers undismayed,
That so her shining honour still might stand:

Here, to tried comrades who have paid full fee
 For England's soul that still is England's own,
 We dedicate a monument of stone . . .
Shall that be all to serve their memory

Nay! If a view may pierce to Paradise,
 They now shall hear in solemn silence vowed
 This pledge:—by naught we do to overcloud
The simple splendour of their sacrifice.

BLESSING UPON A
GLOUCESTERSHIRE VILLAGE

God bless this place of homely inns
And honest workmen supping ale;
Let even farmers' grumbling fail,
And pardon its few sins!

Send, when the great soft curfew bell
Shall dout the light of eyes and houses,
A dream of innocent carouses
And laughter beautiful.

SUNSET

Night shuts from eye of man
    Familiar hills and meadows
Less magically than
    These strange sunset-shadows.

When up that hill I came
    It was not gold, I swear:
And the off horse was lame
    In the team ploughing there.

But now doth the rough world don
    A robe of splendid lies:
Or painfully have I gone,
    And blind, through paradise?

For there, a golden shadow,
    Lieth the little hill.
A smooth purple meadow
    Two golden horses till.

SOLITARY CONFINEMENT

No mortal comes to visit me to-day,
    Only the gay and early-rising Sun
Who strolled in nonchalantly, just to say,
    "Good morrow, and despair not, foolish one!"
But like the tune which comforted King Saul
Sounds in my brain that sunny madrigal.

Anon the playful Wind arises, swells
    Into vague music, and departing, leaves
A sense of blue bare heights and tinkling bells,
    Audible silences which sound achieves
Through music, mountain streams, and hinted heather,
And drowsy flocks drifting in golden weather.

Lastly, as to my bed I turn for rest.
    Comes Lady Moon herself on silver feet
To sit with one white arm across my breast,
    Talking of elves and haunts where they do meet.
No mortal comes to see me, yet I say
"Oh, I have had fine visitors to-day!"

Douai,
August 20th, 1916.

TO THE UNKNOWN NURSE

Moth-like at night you flit or fly
To where the other patients lie;
I hear, as you brush by my door
The flutter of your wings, no more.

Shall I now call you in and see
The phantom vanish instantly?
Perhaps some sixteen stone or worse,
Suddenly falling through my verse!

Nay, be you sour, or be you sweet,
I'd see you not. Life's wisdom is
To keep one's dreams. Oh never quiz
The lovely lady in the street!

I knew a man who went large-eyed
And happy, till he bought pince-nez
And saw things as they were. He died
—A pessimist—the other day.

INVITATION

The silver grass of frosted meadows
        Gleams winterly—
        A frozen sea
Under the moon: and great elm-shadows
        In ebony
        Made deliberately
To the last twig, that light surprise.
        The quiet hour
        Is a flower
Of silver which blooms in paradise.

Come, for your kingdom is here, beloved,
        Reign o'er the hour!
        Pull now the flower
Whose root is far away from earth removed!
Steal like a white moonbeam moving
        O'er the meadows,
        And let shadows
Shield from the world our loving!

THE HOUR OF MAGIC

The moon's pale light
    Maketh a glory
In the cool night;
And little elves
    Dance in it, hoary
With sparkling frost;
Warming themselves
Till morning drags
    Over the hill
Life in her rags;—
The magic lost.

Dance, little elves
    Your moonlit dance.
Disport yourselves
Sweetly till day's
    Sad circumstance,
Mean fears,
Descend again. Upraise

Your joyous songs,
       Little immortal dreams!
Because time's brazen gongs
Deafen our ears.

A RONDEL OF
GLOUCESTERSHIRE

Big glory mellowing on the mellowing hills,
And in the little valleys, thatch and dreams,
Wrought by the manifold and vagrant wills
Of sun and ripening rain and wind; so gleams
My country, that great magic cup which spills
Into my mind a thousand thousand streams
Of glory mellowing on the mellowing hills
And in the little valleys, thatch and dreams.

O you dear heights of blue no ploughman tills,
O valleys where the curling mist upsteams
White over fields of trembling daffodils,
And you old dusty little water-mills,
Through all my life, for joy of you, sweet thrills
Shook me, and in my death at last there beams
Big glory mellowing on the mellowing hills
And in the little valleys, thatch and dreams.

THE SIGHING MOON

Rose lavish their light upon the dark. The empty room
            Drinks up their perfume.
They will be dead to-morrow, the sweet useless bodies!
            That selfsame goddess
Who peers to-night on maids that lie alone,
            The fruitless moon,
Looks in on them as silverly she moves by,
            And gives a little sigh.

THE FIRST SPRING DAY

(To A. E. S.)

We laid you fast in frozen clay
When Winter had enchained the land.
(Lad, was it but three weeks to-day?)
And now comes Springtime's messenger with golden tidings
    in his hand.

A mist blows off the thawing earth,
And drips from every budding tree,
The springs are loosed, and mad with mirth
Run lisping in the fallen leaves, or laughing in the
    sunlight free.

Oh you who loved the song so well,
Do you not hear the throstle's note?
Nor heed the lovesome light that fell
As warm five thousand years ago, when Solomon, the wise
    king, wrote?

"Sweet," wrote he. Yes, the light is sweet!
And maddening sweet to walk in Spring:
Yet is the pleasure incomplete—
How should the living understand the melodies that dead
     throats sing?

Thinker and poet clutch in vain
The secret of a laughing rill,
And Shakespeare's self could never gain
The message blown so mockingly by trumpet of a daffodil.

Dear lad, for you I will not call,
Nor let a foolish dread be born.
A thousand years is still too small
To learn the secrets you must learn, ere you arise on
     Doomsday morn.

For you have set your ear to earth
To list the growing of the flowers:
And catch the strains of Death and Birth:
And take the honey that is stored by all the flitting
     bee-like hours.

And you must put to memory
The silver music of the stars
That raineth down so silently,
And all the mighty harmony scrolled on the sky in glittering
     bars.

The music that no man can make,
The colours that he cannot see,
These out of darkness you shall take
And nourish up your growing soul with manna of their

mystery.

And then when you awake again
(And I have slept a little too),
How we shall rise to pace anew
An earth—where every dream is true, and nothing is
    unknown but pain.

BEAUTIFUL DREAMING

In fairy dawns
     Of moonlight, silver-cool,
Out upon lovely lawns
     Dances my soul
Beside a lake.

Naked and beautiful
     There dances she
In the silver and cool
     Moonlight, joyously,
Till the day break.

O tragic soul
     That into darkened me
From out that silver-cool
     Moonlight must flee,
When I awake!

O evil dawn

My happy soul to banish!
Making the lovely lawn
     And the moonlight vanish:
And that still lake.

COURAGE

Then suddenly we see who had been blind,
And seeing cast our troubles in the teeth
Of this impostor world, and from its sheath
Draw forth that faery blade long since designed
For dragons. At the close of a troubled day
How often we together sitting in fear
Of trivial terrors by the world brought near
Have laughed as those dread dragons fled away!

And so, doubt not, when living's wheel has run
Its creaking round, vast silence will surge o'er
The alien commands of time and space
Which loud and masterful sounded in the sun:
Then having turned and softly closed the door,
We two shall laugh loud in a quiet place.

THE MOURNING BIRDS

Children shall pluck from off our heads
    A buttercup crown.
Cattle shall eat the emerald robe—
    Death's kingly gown.
Men shall mouth the selfsame words
    Which made a song of love for us.
But 'sweet' and 'sweet' shall cry the birds,
    And doves mourn above for us.

THE DEAD LOVER

It is I.
Know you not why
The sun caresses you,
The wind presses you,
When you awake,
Opening your window at daybreak?

Or why,
When the moon was high,
Her pale beam kissed your throat,
In the hour when the nightingale's note
Entranced
Pale roses, and your heart danced?

Of gleam and shade
Have I made
My body. On the wide
Air doth my spirit ride,
In the sigh
Of midnight trees most nigh.

I, unafraid,
Swift as a falling blade,
With the light and the night
Come to my dreamed delight.
Seek not to fly,
Beloved. It is I.

WINTER MEMORY

Little waves of heat over the ember
  Move, like haze of summer upon a plain
Of golden glowing blossom. (*Heart, remember*
  Thy summer!) Wind and rain,

The winter storm upon my window drumming
  No more I'll hear, let tempest burst its throat.
(*Heart, heed thou nothing louder than bee's humming;*
  A bird's quick slender note!)

THE SKY

Sometimes the sky is like a bell-flower swung
Above the world, sometimes 'tis like a dove
That sits with downy breast our earth above,
Sometimes 'tis like a marble chamber hung
With folded curtains, sometimes it will frown
With angry face, throwing white hailstones down.

At night it's streaked and speckled like an egg
With cloud and blinking stars:—I love it best
That way. For then do purple pools of rest,
Such as envious day in vain may beg,
Island the golden planets deep and deep.
Stars the sky's thoughts are: those still pools its sleep.

KOSSOVO DAY

From this sweet nest of peace and summer blue—
England in June—a sea-bird's nest indeed
Guarded of waves, and hid by the sea-weed
From envious hunter's eye, we send to you
Our flying thoughts and prayers, our treasure too,
Poor though it be to bandage wounds that bleed
For country dear beloved. There the seed
Of homely loves and occupations grew
To wither in the flame of godless might
Kindled by hands of treachery, yet reeking
With blood of friends and neighbours. Serbia, thou
Hast thought us careless and far off; know now
Thy name to us is sudden drums outspeaking
And tortured trumpets crying in the night!*

---

* This poem was sent from Crefeld, but was written in England just before
the author left for the front.

FLOWER O' MAN

All courage of the daffodils
   This chill and sodden month benumbs,
Snow lies bleak on the pointed hills.

Black winds blow, and the rain drums
   Falling from low unfriendly skies.
Hangs back the bravest flower. Here comes

A bud of flesh whose azure eyes
   Taunt the blind heavens: whose tiny voice
Mocks shrill the black wind's miseries.
   Ere golden daffodils rejoice!

EILEEN ANNE

Frond-like your tiny fingers curl,
   Dear baby-girl, around my own.
Fern-like your little life doth twine
        With mine.

Thus Fate may set a green spray dancing,
   Sunnily glancing on a stone,
And wake miraculously some riven wall
        To spring-tide festival.

FOR, WHAT IS MAN?

That curve of shining beauty winding there
  With little ripples fluttering like leaves;
That river, triumphs it upon despair? . . .
  Naught knows it of our life, and nothing grieves.

Nay, but a work of hands; that soaring tower
  Which woos the loveliness of cloud and sun? . . .
Naught recks that either of death's bitter hour,
  Nor grieves for anything done, or left undone.

Beholder, dreamer, maker, man alone
  (More than the thing seen, or the thing made)
Must grieve since he is not as soaring stone,
  Or water flowing down through sun and shade.

Must nurse his sorrow, like a living coal;
  A rebel ever against Time and Chance,
Since God hath blessed his body with a soul,
  And cursed that soul with mortal circumstance.

AT AFTERNOON TEA

We have taken a trench
    Near Combles, I see,
Along with the French.
We have taken a trench.
(*Oh, the bodies, the stench!*)
Won't you have some more tea?
    We have taken a trench
Near Combles, I see.

TO E—

All the busy thoughts that ran
In the brain of this dead man:
All shadowy dreams that heart was dreaming:
Be they mine! So may he shed
Light on that lonely path I tread
Without him. Let his noble scheming
Die not though he be dead!

Thus upon another plot
The planted grain he garnered not
Shall grow, and when those other voices,
His nor mine, at Harvest-tide
Cry their joy both far and wide,
Hid in the crowd that there rejoices,
Content we will abide.

BALLAD OF ARMY PAY

In general, if you want a man to do a dangerous job:—
Say, swim the Channel, climb St. Paul's, or break into and rob
The Bank of England, why, you find his wages must be higher
Than if you merely wanted him to light the kitchen fire.
But in the British Army, it's just the other way,
And the maximum of danger means the minimum of pay.

You put some men inside a trench, and call them infantrie,
And make them face ten kinds of hell, and face it cheerfully;
And live in holes like rats, with other rats, and lice, and toads,
And in their leisure time, assist the R.E.'s with their loads.
Then, when they've done it all, you give 'em each a bob a day!
For the maximum of danger means the minimum of pay.

We won't run down the A.S.C., nor yet the R.T.O.
They ration and direct us on the way we've got to go.
They're very useful people, and it's pretty plain to see
We couldn't do without 'em, nor yet the A.P.C.
But comparing risks and wages,—I think they all will say
That the maximum of danger means the minimum of pay.

There are men who make munitions—and seventy bob
    a week;
They never see a lousy trench nor hear a big shell shriek;
And others *sing* about the war at high-class music-halls
Getting heaps and heaps of money and encores from
    the stalls.
They "keep the home fires burning" and bright by night
    and day,
While the maximum of danger means the minimum of pay.

I wonder if it's harder to make big shells at a bench,
Than to face the screaming beggars when they're crumping
    up a trench;
I wonder if it's harder to sing in mellow tones
Of danger, than to face it—say, in a wood like Trone's;
Is discipline skilled labour, or something children play?
Should the maximum of danger mean the minimum of pay?

COME NOW TO SLEEP

Come now to sleep,
　　To the home of all we crave
To keep, but never can keep
　　This side of the grave.

Come to a land
　　Wherein we may foretaste
All that with heavy hand
　　The sun lays waste.

Come fearlessly: for though
　　His mailed fist strike to shiver
The dream to which we go,
　　It abideth for ever.

THE YELLOW LEAF PRESS CLASSICS SERIES

Leaves of Grass by Walt Whitman ISBN: 1956716203

Chicago Poems by Carl Sandburg ISBN: 1956716122

As a Man Thinketh by James Allen ISBN: 1956716181

Harmonium by Wallace Stevens ISBN: 1956716165